THE TRUTH OF LIFE

HEATHER DELANEY

authorHOUSE®

AuthorHouse™
1663 Liberty Drive
Bloomington, IN 47403
www.authorhouse.com
Phone: 1 (800) 839-8640

Published by AuthorHouse 03/26/2019

ISBN: 978-1-7283-0305-5 (sc)
ISBN: 978-1-7283-0312-3 (e)

Print information available on the last page.

This book is printed on acid-free paper.

INTRODUCTION

Heather has been chosen to help bring our words in to physical form for a number of reasons. She has asked to help this world move forward, she has chosen to embrace and develop her gift of hearing, seeing and feeling both sides of the true world in order to help other spirits understand that they as well have the ability to be present in both sides of the world at the same time. Her life has been designed in a way that she has not been in contact with many like spirits that have her ability in order to keep the words and messages contained in this book clear and uninfluenced. It is with this openness and willingness to accept our words and channel this book for all that we hope you will understand the importance of the messages that are contained within. All of these principles are meant to be simple direct and to empower you with the knowledge that you have the ability to be present in your true life and the truth that is contained within living it.

In the writing of this book we have used the terms "us" and "we" often. The reason for this is because the spirits that are guiding Heather in this work have lived many full life cycles so we can accurately speak from a true place of understanding. We have a clear perspective from both physical vessel form and spirit form. It is important that the spirits on the earth (you) understand that we have direct knowledge of the struggles that you encounter while on your journey. When we speak of God, we do not refer to any man-made religion, culture or mindset it does not matter. It is simply however you think of the creator of the universe. It makes no difference. They are, in fact, all one and the same. It is what resonates with your spirit that is important. We choose to use the title God as it fits for the purposes that are needed to understand at this time. Again, we do not speak of any specific God or religion. He/She is so much greater than any of those one thoughts or concepts. When you see the title, just think of the being that resonates the most with your spirit.

We have been given many names in the past according to how the spirits in the body form (collective) were able to comprehend us. As you will see in reading this book, we no longer need to be separated in your minds. It is time that you believe in the knowledge that we are all connected as one and that we are truly one family created together and working together. Think of us as your brothers and sisters and not as higher beings. We work with you and live with you every day, every breath, and in every cell. This true family lives under the same guiding rules, principles, flow of energy and world. Please embrace us as we have always embraced you.

CHAPTER ONE

Someday, somewhere, somehow, there is a truth that we will all know. It will be undeniable, irreproachable, and unbelievable. That is what this book is about.

The truth about life is not about what it means to exist but what existing means. We all have different ideas, loves, passions and beliefs about what this world should be and become. The interesting part about this is that we have all known what the truth is from the moment we set a tiny foot on this earth. We are all tied together bound by love, compromise, and interests, which are in abundance so much so that it baffles the infinite knowledge that we have when we come to this plain.

This book has taken many years to come together in spirit. There are many different entities that are working in collaboration for this book to come in to being. This has been such a vast collection of knowledge that needs to come through to this world that it over takes even us as we try to have it be processed in a format which all can understand. The world is at a moment in time of rebirth and re-acknowledgement of spirit in the simple understanding of the truths in this life. The world has made things more complex than the Designer had put in place. This is not to say that things are not unfolding according to His will. However, it is unfolding at a much faster pace than we had prepared for. When I say "we," I mean the spirits that are helping to guide this world and its growth. We are a part of God. Always have been and always will be. You are a part of God, no matter what the faith, understanding or intellectual prowess that you have in this life. The simple truth is that we are all together, united as one, in the interwoven electrons, light and electricity which allows us to be. The knowledge we are attempting to impart the world will vary from love, compassion, sacrifice, treatment of others to treatment of self. The most important is treatment to others and self. In this way can you know your own spirit, foster its ability to grow, nurture your true self and those around you.

Yes, I did say compromise. Compromise is at the root core of our bodily experience. We must modify what our spirit in free form knows and what our balance is with body. We must compromise at times to make an equal balance not only at our cellular level. For example, we compromise when we only eat one slice of chocolate cake, when we would rather take it all. We compromise in our relationships. This is NOT a negative. This is to help the other person to grow. Many times we think that compromise is surrendering or giving in. On the contrary; it is a truly loving gift that we give to not only our-selves, but to those around us we love. In the true spirit of compromise, we show love and allow for the freedom of growth. The hardest spiritual thing in this world is to watch a loved one stop growing in spirit-self, and on one's path. For those who are spiritually aware we can see how the light changes from within when they turn away from their life lessons.

Children are not children. They are simply a spirit starting the process of learning again. Reincarnation is, in fact, the most effective tool that God has for us. This has been done over and over again by each of us and will never end as we keep moving forward to that evolutionary and inevitable path that is set before us. Just as the water evaporates, then, transforms and comes back to earth as water again, eventually, so do our spirit selves. Yes, all of this has been communicated before and will again, we are attempting to get the simple understanding out and in to the world. The simplicity of life is what is missing at this point in time. The most neglected and misunderstood connection is that between science and spirit. That is an area which we will discuss in great detail.

When you look into the eyes of an animal, you see balance, harmony, self-love, self-sacrifice, and we think how simple and easy their life is. It can be the bird, the squirrel, the jackal, or the elephant. It does not matter. What we see in their eyes is the simple acknowledgment and understanding of the truth of life. It is us who make it so complicated. Why is it that when we see a young person or an animal hurt it tugs at our hearts more than others? Is it because we believe they are so innocent in this life and that hurt is so unjust? It is because they see the simple truth and understand how immense the hurt truly is. It is not just the hurt to that individual spirit, but how it affects all of the balance when an unjust hurt is caused. What we are seeing and connecting with is their spirit and the enormity of the hurt that has been caused to the balance and order of the spirit world which in turn directly impacts the physical world. It is because they are closer to their full connection of spirit-self than most of the world. Animals carry their direct connection with spirit-self at all times. They are able to be free, love freely, and show a purpose in this world that most of us are unable to grasp. It is that spirit connection that draws us in and allows us to see through the disconnect that we have as we begin the true tests of life. Or, in other words, the lessons and learning curves that we need to go through while here in this life and plain of existence to achieve higher spiritual self.

The world that you live in of today is full of so many vast untapped secrets and knowledge it is hard not to laugh at the innocence of the world. You have computers; you have medicine; you have all of the tools to put the pieces together, but the majority turn away from the simple truth in front of them. That simple truth is that life goes on in spite of all of the work that is being done against it; the tugging, the pulling, the misunderstanding, the over-complications, the hurt, the anger, the war. The simple truth is when you look into the eyes of a child, a dog, an animal or the vast beauty of the earth, you are looking at God and, in turn, all of the spiritual beings and energy that has ever been or ever will be created. The world needs to humble itself in order for true progression of self to take place.

We see the world starting to heal. We see it in the openness of mind and spirit that is starting. We see it in the understanding that is being imparted to the beings coming back and that is why it is now that the time is right for this book to be possible. It is the truth of spirit knowledge that needs to be imparted to those who will take the time to look, see, and feel the difference that it makes in this world. The spirit knowledge that we speak of is simply the knowledge that we all know when we are in spirit form. Spirit form is the exact state of being in which God has created us. We recognize each spirit that we come in contact with; let it be a tree, a grain of sand, or an old animal that we have known many many times before. When we speak of the "common" things of this world like sand and trees they each have their own spirit it is a life force that we recognize and connect with. At one time or another we have each been in direct contact with that energy because we are all made up of it. When we speak of science we are talking about the molecular level. At the molecular level we are tied together with every single being and entity on this earth: every single cell, organism and life force. We are tied together with the earthly body we inhabit and are entrusted with from God and the spiritual fabric that is interwoven in between. Think of a fabric of tightly woven cloth, the colors all melding together to create a new color. That is what the spirit world and the physical world are: One. Each is just as important as the other to create balance and understanding. For without this physical world, we would not be able to move forward in the spirit world. It is the connecting of the two that the world does not understand and the importance that this body experience has on moving us forward.

So many times we see spirits here on earth learning lessons, but they are not able to connect the physical and the spiritual. There needs to be a greater understanding of how immeasurable this bodily experience is. When you think of medicine and the ability that you have to heal yourselves with surgical procedures, medicine, and even in meditation, it baffles us and humbles us at the same time. You are being guided from God when these break throughs take place.

Remember that God has dispatched help for you on your path. You have Spirit Guides who are among you and move with you during this life. You have a Guardian (*in the past we have called them Guardian Angels*) and you have Guiders (*what we have called Angels*).

The most readily misunderstood are your Guiders (*Angels*) and your Guardian (*Guardian Angel*). Your Guardian is with you ever moment you are on this earth. They love you, cry with you, and guard you in no way that you can imagine. They have seen you grow in this life, grow in spirit, and have protected you every step of the way. At times if they deem necessary, they will call for a second Guardian to assist in your protection. This second Guardian will come from the spirit side to assist. Your Guardian's energy is constantly felt as they never leave your side. It is easy to dismiss them as not being there because you have always had their presence with you. The love and power they yield is immeasurable. It is what God has created them to do. Their purpose and driving desire is to protect you and allow you to find your way along the path that you have chosen. They are vigilant and understand how important it is that you are allowed to maintain your freedom of choice while on your journey. It is important that you understand that this bond they have with you is great and that both of you chose each other before you embarked on this journey. Many times you will choose to have the same Guardian with you while during your learning cycle. The bond that is forged between a spirit and a Guardian is unbreakable. Remember to call upon them when you are afraid, talk to them, and allow their energy to be felt by you. These beings are part of God just as you are and allowing them to help you and acknowledging them will assist both of you with the energy that it creates.

Your Guiders (*Angels*) have always been Guiders, that is how God made them and they never change. They have never been part of the physical world as you are. Their task is to help a spirit to develop the gifts which God has given them and when necessary to assist a spirit in physical body healing. You bring to this world all of the knowledge good and bad from past lives within your spirit. The physical body is not able to tap into that complete spirit knowledge, so you no longer fully possess the knowledge that you have. If you have not completed a task or a learning process from another life, you carry it forward to learn. Guiders can help with healing a wrong or a pattern, which a spirit has been carrying over many life times. A spirit can become stuck on a particular lesson. Many times God will make the lesson grow larger in scale while you are on earth to try and get a spirit to overcome that block. It is always easier to deal with it on a small scale, but it becomes necessary for the path that spirit is on to overcome the hurdle and lovingly, God keeps reminding them to deal with that issue. At times, He dispatches Guiders; usually, more than one, to help with this learning. When you think of Guiders, do not think of Angles in the sense that you have been taught by man. They are not far away beings that are intangible to you. Just like your Guardians, they have been dispatched by God to help you while in this physical existence. Do not think of them as beings which are God-like and that you are not worthy to call upon them. God has created you in his image and has provided Guiders to help you move forward on the path which He has set down for you. Again, it is important now in the spiritual development that you stop thinking of them as ethereal creatures and look at them as those who are assisting God and teaching you on his behalf. In the course of your time on earth, you will have many different Guiders depending on what task is set before you at that moment. Sometimes they wish to let you know that they are around and other times they keep silent.

Spirit Guides are very simple in their approach to helping you. Their name demonstrates this as their only purpose is to help you to move forward in learning the spiritual lessons that you have chosen to come to body form to understand. They simply guide you on your spiritual path. This is a very serious responsibility that they take on with great motivation, energy and commitment. These beings have been to the earth and lived many life cycles, just as you. The difference is that they have moved on to a place that they no longer require to come and learn in body form. God has blessed them with the task of watching over their brothers and sisters and witnessing the growth of their spirits. You may have known these beings at one time or another. However, clearly understand that these beings have not been in body form during your current life cycle.

We would like you to realize that the spirit lives endlessly and that those whom God has chosen to be your Spirit Guides have the experience and spiritual learning that goes with the immense task of guiding you here in physical form. Think about how vulnerable your spirit is when it is in physical form. Not that harm will come to your spirit, but the fact is that you have forgotten all of the knowledge that you have gained in living those other life cycles and the knowledge that you have gained in full spirit form. Those watching over you understand that there is no greater task than to help guide you back to your true self and that not just God, but you as well, have placed your faith in them to guide, guard and assist you.

Each Spirit Guide has an area in which they excel. During your life, they will be a part of every action that you choose. They are able to help encourage you when you require it. Do not misunderstand. They do not make choices for you. Only you have that ability for yourself. No one else does. As you move along your path in the lifecycle one Spirit Guide may move away while a new one comes in to work with you. It depends on what you require at that moment on your path. It is a seamless exchange to you and you are never left alone. In fact, Spirit Guides work as a unit. They are never working with a spirit individually. They work as a collective; each providing their own area of knowledge and energy. Think of a wonderful symphony and how each individual instrument moves together to create a new and wondrous sound. Each instrument has its own sound, and notes to play, but they all combine together to bring beauty and harmony within a piece. That is what Spirit Guides do collectively with a spirit. They provide the harmony to the music while the spirit itself is the conductor.

CHAPTER TWO

THE FIRST BROTHER

"The world as it turns wildly in space has been directly pulled and shaped as the sand by the water." This was said many life-times ago to me as I was in body form. Yes, as a Guider of the earth, I as you walked the earth with others. In order for God to give us the task of watching over and guiding the development of spirits on this earth, we had to experience it fully as well. It was so long ago it is hard to imagine at times, but being in this spirit form, I am able to recall all when I wish, especially the sea. I am still pulled and directed to that area as my brother is pulled and directed to the wind, or what he calls "sky mountains", and the other to the fires within the earth. The three of us are to watch over the growth of the earth and those spirits within it. We have a very different role than the Guiders that you have directed by God, that have always been and will only be Guiders. We had to develop along our spiritual path for many, many cycles in order to be ready to Guide the earth. We needed to fully understand the feeling, walks and struggles that take place while in body form. This is why we are able to talk so easy with you about it. We lived it many times over. There is a true connection between spirit-self, body and earth. Do not confuse this with mind-body spirit. When we speak of body, that includes the mind, but not the spirit; and the earth are the other life forces of energy that co-exist with us all.

We have already told you that we are all connected in the woven fabric of energy. Now, look at it as if it were a pond. When one energy ripple is made, it flows outward in all directions. This is true when an unjust hurt occurs. It is true that a spirit in and of itself cannot be hurt in the physical sense, in your way of thinking. However, it can feel the emotional hurt in a much more profound way. When you start magnifying the collective hurt that is caused, the energy flow grows and grows until a wave is created and then it can keep growing until it is pulled apart by another energy that has been created that is of equal or greater strength. Energy, positive and negative, are at the core of all existence in spirit-self and body. Why do you think it is so hard on the body when you choose to go against your spirit-self in a learning lesson? Why do you think that you give yourselves cancer, stress and other forms of bodily injury?

As time has gone on, the injuries that you inflict on your body change in alignment with the spiritual learning you under-go. As the path you are on grows higher and higher, so does the nature of the ailment that you give to yourselves. It is all energy that is redirected in to an anti-functional stream. The world will turn as the energy in you turns and moves outward and back inward if you allow it. The true flow of energy is outward from spirit. In your true spirit form this energy never ceases to stop flowing. It is a constant in the existence and immovable. On earth in body form there is a struggle between the energy within the spirit and the energy within the body. If you are able to keep the balance between them, you possess the attributes of both, however, it is rare that you are able to sustain this. This IS by design, for if you are able to keep the equal balance of both you would not learn the lessons that you need to so readily. Again, God has given you direct, step by step, within self and within the spirits around you to put the balance back again. It is a constant struggle and one that moves you forward in the spiritual thirst of self that nurtures and guides you on your spiritual path on earth and ultimately to a greater spiritual understanding of all.

The sea shows all of its essence. It does this by the movement of the waves, the white at the top, the blue in the deep, and the animals within. When calm, the creatures emerge to the top and you see the glimpse of their beauty, and are in awe of their harmony, and grace. Your spirit in body shows itself in the ripples of the energy that emerge from your body when it is in power; the color of the energy that is disbursed from within and the cells of the body that have been created as a means of experience for the spirit to move forward. Just as when the sea shows the glassy tranquil mirror on the top, the body shows the glow of sunlight and balance when it is in harmony with body and moving on its spiritual path on earth. When it is disrupted, the energy becomes unsteady, abrupt, and agitated resulting in physical and emotional pain that casts a ripple to all of those around to feel the energy. As does the sea when a storm erupts and disperses the waves and sends the creatures to the bottom for safety. When the sea is angry and at unrest, all the creatures know it. When the spirit is at unrest and not in full power, all of the cells in the body know it and move to seek shelter from the uneven energy. If this does not cease, then it will result in the cells becoming displaced or in other words; sick. By not following the path that God has set us on you become dysfunctional in your own lives, in the lives of others, and ultimately in your body. A vast array of healers have been dispatched to the earth to help bring to light this connection by healing. We wish to acknowledge that these spirits are working for the greater good and will continue to do so. Just look and you will find them.

We encourage you to continue to understand the relationship between true spiritual path and illness. When in balance, the energies are in harmony and you will not crave the foods that are not able to sustain your body. It is the imbalance of spirit that causes these cravings. When you seek to control the environment around you and not live within the confines of the world that God has created for you in that moment, you are disrupting the energy flow around you. This is a result of trying to control the world. When you think about it, how could you control God? In essence, when you try to control your world you are trying to do just that: control God's plan or will. The more you try, the more and more you are pulled away from the spiritual goal you are here to obtain. This is a very simple theory, but it is extremely hard in practice. God knows this and provides, moreover, surrounds you with the beings in spirit form and on earth to assist you to stay on your path. Some of you are able to see the signs clearly and move forward with direction and understanding while others need to be taught to do so, or at least they feel as though they need to be taught. They simply need to be reminded of the truth that they already know. This life is a spiritual journey with a set pattern and road map that they themselves helped to develop while in spirit form. Just as with any journey there is a plan, directions and those along the way to help point the way. You just have to be open to asking for directions.

CHAPTER THREE

THE SECOND BROTHER

The days seem long, the nights cold, but that is the way that it is in the desert. When I walked the earth long periods ago, this is what it was like for me. I am now a higher spirit, one who guides the earth, and those who are here to find their spiritual path and journey. My brothers and I have been doing this for a long time, but to you it would be nothing. In the amount of time that we have guided you it would be so small a period to you that you could not grasp the concept in physical form.

My brother talks about the sea and the water. I like to use fire. The reason why is that under the earth you have molten lava, that is the area that resonates with me. No, fire is not harmful in itself. It is how it is used and directed. It can either cleans and purify or burn and destroy. My job is to guide it for the correct purposes.

It is of no surprise that we are all made up of energy and molecular biology. What you need to understand is that we have the power over all. Not in the sense that you think of God's power, but in the understanding that if you choose to manipulate your energy you have control over your own lives. My brother explained how illness becomes so vast in your time here on earth. How easy it is to understand why you become ill, but he has not informed you how easily it is corrected. Yes, you have healers to help those of you who need it, while others need to just meditate and focus on that energy which is created in between the cells and shift it towards the light and good. That is what I do when I work with the earth's mantle and structure. These shifts in energy between cells are very important and create massive changes within the body. When you hold on to hurt, especially unjust hurt, then it creates a rift between the cells which needs to erupt out into the world as you know it. Just as a mantle shift causes the disbursement of gasses and other powerful energies to move the earth's surface, that is exactly what is happening within your cells. If you allow the energy flow to stay stagnate, it will ultimately erupt into a full illness that you can see from the outside. When I push the energies to a point within the earth's core at a certain time, it must move to the surface. If you hold in the energy hurt, it will need to come to the surface. It can take many forms depending on the location that the hurt resides in. Just like the pressure I create within the earth, it is directed to a specific point on the earth surface. It is not just a random act. Please just look at this as a comparison with energies and not a means to punish people. That is NOT what happens when you think about disasters that take place. We will discuss that specifically later on in this book. For now; I want you to think of the energy and the pictures that I am attempting to have you connect within your minds.

This energy shifting is very powerful and you can accomplish a tremendous amount in life if you understand how to utilize it. Yes, I utilize this on a vastly larger scale. However, the outcome is the same as to what you are capable of doing within your own cell structure, but it will ultimately come out in a positive way if you use it for the right reasons within your body. Just as you have the power and ability to heal you have the power and ability to hurt as well. When you choose to hold onto hurts that are not truly associated with a random hurt or evil act, you are causing self-harm and bodily injury to yourself and to those who love you. What I mean by this is think of all the time you spend pouring over the things you feel someone has done to cause you pain. Each time you look at it over and over again you are pushing that pain back into your body. You are reliving that energy hurt and each time you are sending that energy back into your body and building on it.

Thought gives energy to patterns of things. When you repeat looking at a pattern of hurt that someone has caused to you, then you are amplifying the hurt each time. What you need to do is stop, look at the hurt, and decided if you own it or not. What that means is simple. Did I cause hurt to the other person in order for them to hurt me? If the answer is no, then you must forgive that person and understand that they are on their own spiritual journey and for that moment in time there was a lesson to be learned either by you or them. If you can see the lesson, then you can let go of the hurt and purify it from your energy being. If you keep looking at it you are pushing that energy to a point where ultimately it will need to erupt and as you know that is not beautiful when it comes to the body.

God did not make your vessel to handle these energy irruptions for any length of time. He did, however, use it within the earth as a means to grow and change the outer layers. Try to understand that the energy disruptions that you have within the body are also a way of protection. That energy needs to flow outward. You have the choice of letting that energy out in constructive manners or holding it in and then the energy will find its own way to release. This can be harmful to yourself and those who are around you. It can be as simple as suddenly erupting in anger or physical negative actions. It can be a surge of energy release that makes you have an uncontrollable desire to move your body. The one thing that is constant is that this energy must move out of the body in one fashion or another. It is your choice as to how it flows out. Either in constructive or deconstructive ways. The critical path to understanding how these energies flow is allowing yourself to be open and to watch the living things around you. How the birds fly and how the earth moves. How the water flows and the sun rises; always in constant motion. The air bends the trees, the flowers, and the people. It is not so different within your own bodies. The difference is that your mind controls the movement of energy within your body. Your spirit allows for the control and movement of your thoughts within the body and mind combination. When you are in balance with your spirit-self then you are able to easily balance the energies that are moving between your cells. What I mean by this is that being in touch with your spirit-self allows you to have better control as to how you react to situations and thus the type of energy that is being created and released within your body.

You should equate balance with peace, harmony, growth and control.

I know that this is not an easy process for you to understand at this time, but if you can stretch your mind to encompass so much more than just what you believe it is, your existence will become much easier. Stop and think of the earth. How the land is surrounded by the sea. Think of the land as the body self and the water as the spirit-self energy. The water on the earth reaches out and connects all of the land masses together. In this same way, the spirit energy connects all of the physical bodies together. That water encompasses the entire earth all reaching and touching at once. This is how the combined spirit energy is. Always touching and moving together as one. At times different currents are pulling one way, but ultimately whatever touches that water on one side of the earth moves and flows to the other, and in turn it is so with the collective spirit energy that is here on this planet at one time. It even moves out in to other dimensions, but that is for another discussion. Think now of how that disruption in the ocean moves to the land. If it is harsh and strong it will impact the land in a seemingly negative way, this is the same when it comes to an unjust hurt. The energy then erupts out of the body and moves in to the spirit energy collective and affects all of the flow. When you take in to account all of the spirits on the earth at one time and all of the experiences that they have good and bad you can start to imagine the energy waves that are created that affect all of the collective energy.

The land and the sea are connected by the entire center of the earth. Within the earth I can manipulate the energy to create new areas within it. Take this one step further.

Think of the earth as one single body and spirit-self. The land is the body and the water is the spirit-self of the earth. The earth spirit-self is made up of all of the collective spirit energy that is released from all of those beings on earth at one time. The energy flow that is created positive and negative directly affects the body (the earth). If it is negative, the earth absorbs and holds that energy in until it then must be released and the earth core is cleansed. It will then erupt allowing for that negative energy to escape. The earth absorbs the energy that all of the spirits here are releasing. It is my job to help the earth to utilize the energy that it absorbs in ways that are going to help move forward the paths which God has set down at that time for all beings on the earth. Your combined energies help to dictate what and how the earth will respond. When the earth needs to release energies, what God asks me to do is help the earth to release this in the way that He feels is most beneficial for the learning of those spirits on the earth. This can be positive or negative. It can be destructive or cleansing depending on how an individual chooses to look at it. These are earth lessons that affect multiples of beings at the same time. Each of you knows this and understands this on a spirit-self level. We are all connected and tied together in spirit energy, in spirit-self, in the physical bodies, and the earth that you are walking on.

It is time that you start to understand that all are one and none are separate. Many times before we have explained the idea that the body and spirit are one. That you can tap into that knowledge and understanding if you are willing to follow the path you are set here for. What is not readily understood is that the earth is just as much a spirit-self as any of you are. It is a whole being entity that God created to assist you while on this spiritual journey He has set forth. It reflects the notions, movement and attributes that the collective energies inhabiting it are feeling. In order for you to truly reach a level of understanding you must first understand yourself and the enormity of the role in which you play in the universe.

The cycle of the spirit path on earth can be short or long, difficult or easy, depending upon how much knowledge you wish to utilize. Yes, each time you come you are on another spiritual journey that may repeat the root lesson. The struggle is not to overly focus your attention on just self or just the collective. It is to draw the comparison and balance between. You come with like-minded individuals who are trying to move forward on their own journey while at the same time to assist you. They may be assisting you by creating a sense of urgency within you or a sense of escape from them; all of this is a lesson and equally as important.

The toughest lessons that move us forward on our path and in life are the ones which we struggle the most inwardly. They are the spiritual struggles that we must learn and understand to move forward. It is the dire need to be loved, wanted and shown that you matter. It can be the feelings of abandonment at an early age. Each one of us moves forward at our own pace, with our own knowledge and inner struggle with spirit-self. God has created you to be strong, fit and full of energy. When that energy becomes low all that is required is to be still within one's self and tap in to the energies around. Your spirit energies do not just feed yourselves, but the earth and they are the means in which the earth has to sustain itself. Without your energy the earth itself would cease to be. Your will, desire, and spirit-self feed the earth. The choice on how you use your energy is not just for your own self-preservation and health but that of the earth.

Animals and plants on the earth know this and utilize the life energy that they have in conjunction with the earth. They never worry, fear, or spend useless energy. They simply know what to do and how to sustain themselves when left to their own devices. It is when an individual chooses to act counter to what they know is appropriate and fitting for that life force. For example; when harm is caused to an animal or plant in this world. Yes, some plants and animals are used for food. This is not what we are speaking of. Those, when done appropriately, are for just cause and do not add negative energy into the earth or the spirit energy which intern reaches out to affect all. Animals know what their role is on this earth and understand that death is part of it. They do know the difference when it is for a purpose or from an unjust motivation.

It is the unjust hurts that are caused by choice and are a result of not being in touch with your spirit selves. It is what we see at times, the blatant turning away from what the spirit-self knows is just and right and letting other influences direct you. These are the unjust hurts of this world that we must get you to understand how horrible they are. They can be simple or astonishingly complex, but it all starts with a choice not to listen to your spirit-self. When an injury is purposely caused to an animal, it shows in their eyes, in their energy being, and ripples out in waves. It is this energy, that an individual who is completely away from God's path for them thrives on. It is like a drug that they grow on with the negative energy that this unjust hurt creates. The same happens when a child is hurt. These are not topics that I care to dwell on, the thoughts of them hurt all and even the discussion goes to the core of us all. The world must understand what it is doing to itself. Even when you are on God's path for yourself you have choices at times that will release a type of energy. Stop and think about what type of energy will be released in to the world both physical and spiritual. There is no such thing as a little harm. Once the energy is created, it must go someplace and it will combine with other energy that has been released.

Think of the power that the combined collective energy has, for example, fear. When fear is being generated from individuals, it grows and the only way it is controlled or squelched is by you as an individual. Only you can control that reaction within yourself with the grace of God. You are able to decide how you will react to a situation and not just in the context of right and wrong or good and evil. Think of the end result with the energy production. Now you understand how the earth feeds upon the collective energy as a spirit-self. Do not just think how will my actions be viewed by God, but what type of energy am I going to disburse to all others and the life planet that I reside on. The world has been focused on what God will think and this is only a part of the equation. It is time that you now begin to fully understand the other side of that equation and that is the science of the energy and how that ultimately impacts your life, your world and those that follow. God does not send down a hurricane, flood or earthquake to teach you a lesson. It is simply a by-product of what the life energy on the earth has created with the choices they have made. It is a result of your own doing. Yes, there are times when energy within and around the earth are released as a cleansing purpose to keep the earth body balanced. This happens constantly and with no major impact to you. It is just accepted as the science of the earth. This is true, but when a major catastrophe takes place this is a result of the energy that has been pushed in to the earth needing to escape. There is only so much negative energy that can be absorbed without a consequence.

The earth was constructed to handle an appropriate amount of energy and with the science that you have constructed in your own minds it is disbursed in a seemingly reasonable way and accepted by you. This is very important and necessary. What you must consider now is that the release that is drastic and over-powering resulting in what you deem random acts of weather are not this at all. It is the buildup of negative unjust energy that has to be released. When you are sent here on your spiritual path, it is not always just for your own growth, but it is also for the greater good.

At different times on each of our paths, we are used to help move others forward in their growth. This is a truly wonderful and loving gift that is by design. We are all connected in our lessons and our movement of energy. At one time, you may choose to have a short life span here in order to move a loved spirit forward more quickly on their path. This is by design with both spirits in full knowledge. When a great loss occurs with many people at the same time, this is something that was designed as a teaching tool for the spirit selves to move forward as a collective. If God did not balance the good and bad energies on the earth then the bodily experience would be useless as a learning ground.

It is time to move you forward with the thought process and understanding that what you do, how you do it, and your free will choices all affect the spirit-self collective, the energy in which it moves, and the earth. This is not a different concept. Most of you have this connection and can feel the truth behind this; however, this book is for those of you who are just starting to look at this and understand the overall reaching truth of life that we are all beings, whether in spirit form or in spirit-body form, directly linked together impacting and manipulating each other. This is very basic. It is the essence of what science is based on positive and negative, attraction and reaction. These are the simple principles that God has given you to work with in your mind. They make sense to you, are easily constructed and adapted to each situation relating to the earth.

The leap that you must make now is that it is the same in the spirit world and we are all bound by the energy and the same principles. Just because some of you are not able to see the energy movement, you can feel it. Those of you who do see it must start to speak in a more profound way. It is time that those who understand this connection and have done the science or have the gift of seeing this energy movement have the responsibility to share it with the world. It is critically important that this link be made, that the collective begins to accept this as truth. You will find more and more of the scientific world will continue to demonstrate the movement of energy and a new technology will become prevalent that will help dismay any thoughts of this movement of energy as theoretical. It has been proven, and will be again with a new technology which will assist in the forward movement of this connection in thought, so the world will move to a new level of acceptance. It will take time for this to become common in the thoughts of those on earth; however, it is imperative that the shift continue on a progressive momentum. This book will touch on many different concepts on an overreaching scale. This is the first to just start you thinking and re-evaluating how you look at the complete world. The complete world being the spirit and body experience combined. No longer thinking of it as separate with the spirit world affecting the bodily world, they work in tandem and cannot be separated. The only unchangeable energy that has been created is that from God. Once the energy has been created, it is in constant movement and never destroyed. It just changes form. From spirit energy to body/spirit energy back to spirit energy again. The by-products are absorbed by the earth and then returned back to the universe for creative purposes, it is a never ceasing cycle.

As the world seems to change endlessly, the universe is more of a constant in your minds. Yes, for many it seems to expand and contract as with the will of God. It really is not, it is constant with energy, as you will discover in time. It is the shifting of the energy that God's will impacts. The energy just changes form, whether it be on the earth, another planet, or in the vast universe. The one thing that God has made constant is the amount of energy that has been dispatched for the use in the spiritual and physical realms. The energy just moves back and forth between the two. One affects the other. It takes energy for your Spirit Guides, Guardians and Guiders to work with you. It takes energy for you to get up in the morning and put into thought what a beautiful day it is. It takes energy thought to decide to be happy or sad. It takes energy thought to choose to follow ones path or to walk away from it.

All things take energy to move forward and to be. The more you are in touch with your spirit-self and the true path that you are here to walk, the less energy it takes to make it through the daily struggles here in this body form. It is the shedding of the will of man that takes the most energy. When you are fighting what you know is right and true to obtain something that is your own will and not that of God's, you are using the most energy. When you think about the energy that you have in body form and, if you choose to utilize it in a direct counterproductive way how much energy is wasted compared to where that energy should be to keep you balanced. It is not just the body chemistry and how your cell structure has been put together by God that impacts the balance you have within. It is the choices that you make and how you utilize the energy. Quite simply - how you decide to use your energy power. This choice is something that we have while here on earth and struggle with. It is the most singular destructive and productive means that you have while in body form. Energy power is simple, easily tapped into, and the strongest that you can ever hope to command. When the spirit and physical body combine, it results in an individual's peace, harmony, balance and strength. It is the most loving gift that you can give to yourself. Like anything, it is a conscious choice to move toward this state of being. It is achievable and attainable for all. God has worked with each of you to put into place a path that will help you to achieve this. One person's path will be completely different from another's according to how much spiritual growth they have set out to accomplish in this life.

Energy power is the energy that God has provided you with while in body form. It is that energy you command in personal thought and personal action. The way you move this energy power out from within is a result of the decisions you make while living your life here on earth. The danger lies in the decision itself. Whatever decision is made your energy power will move outward. Remember everything is connected and all energy will ultimately ripple out and touch everything in the physical, spiritual and outer worlds. I have already taught you how the collective energy impacts the earth.

The spirit word is made up of light and energy and can be easily seen and felt by all. There are many who are able to work with both the physical and spiritual world. They are of course connected as my brother and I have been attempting to demonstrate in the sections leading up to this. The difficult thing that many of you have in accepting is that these two worlds are in actuality one. It is the ability to open your mind and allow your spirit connection to flow completely through the body to enable your seeing, hearing and feeling of the two worlds. Once you are able to accept that these two work as one, the ability to move through this life does become easier. It is still a constant struggle because the mind will continue to challenge what the body eye cannot see until that first leap of faith has been confirmed. This is accomplished when what you see, hear and feel unfolds in your own life. It is different when you see it take place in other's lives, but when it happens in your own it moves you in to a completely different state of being. One which you must continue to look at and accept. It is very easy to get pulled out of the balanced state to that of the seemingly mundane issues of the world around you. It is keeping the balance on an ongoing basis that is the work. It is continuous while you are in body form and with anything the more you practice and focus on it the more it will become part of who you are in this physical form. It is taking the time to make yourself a priority in a way that will allow you to be there fully for those who are around you and the world in its entirety.

Finding this balance is different for each person. Working with your Spirit Guides can help you to locate the direction to take to assist in this balance. For some, it is discovering the gift that God has given to them and how to best utilize it in this life. For others, it is connecting with the world around them and seeing the balance in the earth. The simplest thing to do is to ask all of those beings who guide you for help. The balancing of energy is also well established by Chakra balancing. This is when a guided assistant is able to help you bring spirit universal energy and human (physical) energy combined to help balance and align the energies within the body. This has been done for many years and is a powerful tool. Of course, there are many things that you can accomplish by yourself by just choosing to live a balanced life. Meditation, music, art or working in a way that utilizes your gift are all examples of how to help find the balance that each of you seeks. At this point, just accept that you are able to balance your life and it is not as difficult as one may think. It is something that you are all capable of doing and achieving.

CHAPTER FOUR

THE THIRD BROTHER

When the world was created, it was set in such a way to help bring about the spiritual changes that need to take place in order to move a spirit into the next level of understanding. It was made with preset balances and the ability to expel energy in the most expedient of ways. Science understands many of these ways including volcanos, storms, earthquakes, geological changes and the adaption that animals make to survive in the ever changing climates. These things may take years to come to pass, but they are all serving the same purpose to release and change the energy within. When you are sent to come back in physical form to learn God does not just use the circumstances that will happen in your life, but also chooses what is happening to the earth at the same time. You may wonder why it can take a spirit an extended period of time to come back to earth in physical form again while others come back quickly. We must all take the time to review the lessons that we have or have not learned in this life, but the spirit chooses not only what time, what people to be with, and the life circumstances. It must also decide under what earth circumstances will help it move forward the most as well. It must find the appropriate time to return in physical form and it can take generations for this to line up according to the set upon lessons that spirit needs to learn. Try to think of time more in spirit physical lives than in the standard manual timeframes you use. Time is exceedingly complex in physical form and utterly the opposite in spirit form.

The growth of a spirit is endless. God has provided an infinite amount of time to work on one's spiritual path. The only time limit that is imposed is that in which the physical body can endure. This can vary from experience to experience. One body vessel may be put together in a way to outlast another if that spirit-self chooses to make choices to prolong that body. Another experience may be for someone to learn the spiritual lesson of how connected the body and spiritual self can be by choosing to cause harm by pushing toxic elements into the body. We all have choices when we are here that affect our spirit selves and our body vessel. Yet another may have a body that no matter how well they take care of it is preset to have illnesses resulting from being unbalanced within which ultimately allows them to move forward in their own understanding of spirit-self. The possibilities are endless and so are the spiritual lessons that we are capable of learning. The only difference is in the way in which we each need to be taught. God is the greatest master of teaching. He will continue to show us the lessons we need to learn in small ways at first and then allow us to choose how difficult we need the lesson to be. Many times we ask why is this lesson so difficult? It is not so much as the lesson is difficult it is that you require the teaching to be strong and overpowering for you to grasp the concept. When you come up against a lesson that is a struggle for you it can simply be that you have been attempting to learn it during several lives and you have carried over the incorrect ways of looking at the problem and the solution. When this happens, it is harder for the spirit to cast off those old repetitive ways of looking at the problem. God does not give up. He just finds other ways of drawing our attention to the lesson we need to learn until ultimately we understand it. We not only have to understand it, but we must successfully apply it while in body form. It is only then that we can move forward.

Moving forward on a spiritual path is the ultimate reason why God created us. We have so many vast areas to learn from the energy movement, the human movement of thought power and the physical ramifications that take place within the earth itself. As you grow, the spirit becomes stronger and lighter with energy. What I mean is that you can actually see the light around the spirit grow more powerful, not in a sharp edge effect, but in a soft loving universal light which we all recognize. Our goal is to grow to a spiritual understanding of universal balance, clarity and self-reliance in the knowledge of how everything is connected. In true spirit form, you do not feel the loss of others you do, however, feel the loneliness of missed opportunities while on the earth. This is what can drive a spirit to stay around a loved one while they are still on earth. They feel as though their job with that person is not finished and they wish to see it through.

Just as we spoke of how we are all connected, you are still connected to those you worked with in physical form once you have returned to spirit form. It is a choice as to how connected you wish to be or to move directly on and continue the spiritual growth process. Most will choose a combination for a while until it is time to come back to physical form. This is why at times you are able to feel the presence of a loved one. They are still around you helping to guide you.

For many the loss of a loved one is the jumping off point of a spiritual growth cycle. It allows them to consider possibilities that they have not taken the time before to see. When you are able to feel the presence of someone that you just lost it touches the direct spirit-self in a way that people are not able to explain, but are also unable to deny. It is that moment of knowing and not requiring "proof" that allows the spirit to connect and balance with the body to come to an acknowledgement that there is something more than just the physical and the two are connected.

I am the third brother and not as eloquent as my other brothers. The wind and the Sky Mountains are my home. It is the place in which all spiritual beings pass to and from the in between sections of the universe that are in constant movement with light, energy, spirit and the universal laws. It is where my humble energy resides to do the work that God has set before me. My work is no more important or profound as the work that God has dispatched each of you to do. It is just at this time my spiritual growth is aimed at understanding the collective and watching over the movement of all. The same as my brothers, just in a different area of the earth. From my perch above I am able to witness the spirit movements of all and witness the connection and bond between both spiritual movement and physical movement. The wind is so much more than just what science has discovered. It is the means in which a spirit can move the energy around them to have a loved one feel their presence. It is the swirl of the leaves and scent of flowers that allows the strong connection of a loved one who has passed. It is the initial means for many to start the connection to a spirit who they have lost recently. It is the way in which a Guider *(Angel)* will call attention to the spirit they are helping. It is simple; it is art; and, it is spirit life movement.

Ezekiel is what I was called when I was a shepherd the last time I was in physical form. I still find myself being drawn to examples of that life. The constant that I see is the beauty of the earth and spirit world combined. When you are able to just sit and watch the flow of the two together, it is more profound than my humble words can ever hope to express. The surge of balance, the correctness of the being, is immeasurable. It fills the spirit with complete acceptance and knowledge that the complete world (spirit and earth) can and should never be changed. The balance between the two are constantly being reset and clarified by all beings each moment. It is this balance that is so awe inspiring to me.

My job is very simple and not as profound as my brothers. I work to allow the flow of energy and movement to match that of the earths. I watch to ensure that the beings moving in between are able to be successful and not caught in energy currents that will take them away from their path that God has set out for them. It is the to and from movements of these beings from earth to spirit and back again. I ensure that the large movement of energies that have been expelled from the earth are moved to the location that God has decided they are best served. This can be moving them into the spirit world or back into the physical world or at times even out beyond. It is where-ever God feels the need for that energy to be at that moment. My brother has already explained that the energy that is expelled by the collective spirits on the earth needs to be moved out of the earth. Once that is done in the fashion that God deems best, it is then up to me to see that it moves on to the next purpose that God has for it. As you know it is never used up, it just merely moves on to the next task that is set for it. Just as the spirit-self energy does not end, it moves on to the next cycle of its existence.

I like to think of my perches as Sky Mountains, funny I know, but as I have told you before, I still feel very close to my physical form that I last had. It helps me to do my work better, truly understanding the challenges and the feeling of being lost when I was in body form. It is not easy for any of us no matter how far along on our spiritual path to be in body form. It is hard, it is lonely, and we all long to be connected with home *(spirit world)* again. I do not say this to discourage you now, but in hope that you will better understand that we all know the challenges that you face, that you endure, and that you must overcome. Each of you is set on your own journey, but draw comfort in knowing that the spirit beside you is doing the same. Be joyful when you are able to walk side by side together as your paths converge and do not think of them as gone when the paths diverge. It is simply they are moving forward on the path they are supposed to even if that brings them to true spirit form before you. Know that the energy you share with them will always be in existence, it never leaves it just changes. It is this changing that is to be celebrated. It is simply one moving forward on the spiritual journey and awakening that we are all undertaking. Yes, even my brothers and I are on our own journey's utilizing the gifts that God has given us after working for lifetimes to perfect them. We are still perfecting the gifts just as you are. The one thing that is different from where I sit and you is that I have had more lifetimes to realize that God gives us many gifts to move us forward. He always adds to them, but never takes them away. You will find that each gift is utilized in each life learning. However, one gift may grow more than others depending on what is set out to be accomplished in that life cycle. I am not just speaking about that spirit-self's lesson, but those of the collective as well.

The collective may be thought of as complex by my brothers or at least I find their explanations a bit overly stated at times. I am a simple spirit and please pardon me for being so basic. The collective is what I see from above as the combination of all the spirits below. Depending upon what the collective energy is at that given moment the color of it will change. At times, it is orange with healing, green with growth, white/yellow with peace and balance, or dark purple with hurt. By seeing the color of the collective energy below I am able to understand what type of energy release will come and I can prepare for what movement of the energy will be needed. When in healing, it is soft and comforting; when in balance calm and reflective; when in hurt, a cleansing wind to move the energy fast and fierce out and away. It is very basic as is the way to a balanced life. Nothing in the physical life or the spirit world is meant to be complex. It is the simplicity that makes us in physical form disbelieve. It is the simple balance that we see around the physical world. How the stream runs free to the ocean to balance the pond. How the food we eat balances the energy and cells within (when we choose the right ones). How the balance of emotional energy is felt when a mother holds a new child. The feeling of completion when you utilize a gift that God has given you in the correct way. It is all around the world. All you need to do is look or open a science book to see it. It is something that we are all born to do, but we forget how as the struggles put in front of us take us away from our spirit selves and the balance we come to the physical world with.

The general colors of the collective energy from above look more like the cosmos with colors swirling and flecks of light moving together. It is very rare that only one color is visible; it is usually a combination. It is when a color becomes most prominent that I know that I will be called upon to disperse the energies elsewhere. For the most part the wind that you feel is light and love with spirits moving through with very little effort. These beings can be on their way to live another lifetime or they can be stopping to assist a loved one. There are many reasons why a spirit will come back to the physical world and it is part of my responsibility to see that they are able to move freely without being swept up in any collective energy. I am not protecting them as a Guardian protects you, that is not my purpose. It is just to ensure that they are not pulled into the collective energy and end up in another location. You see the collective energy is immeasurably strong and the pull is so magnetic it is easy for the energies of other beings to be swept up in to it. This is what I watch for. As I said, most of the time the energy of the collective is humming along with no assistance required and then it is common place for beings to move around freely. In some ways I am a traffic guard.

The earth is just a reflection of what the spirit-self energies in physical form release. My brothers have touched on this in great detail. The simplicity is that the same connection that you have within your physical body vessel and your spirit-self you have with the earth. It is very simple and basic. The planet's life is that of the body. If we choose to put negative harmful items into it, then it will take on a negative balance and the energy will be released in negative ways from the cell structure of the planet. If we choose to put well balanced nutrients in, it will flourish. I know you may be thinking "why do I need to hear this yet again?", but you do because what we are wishing to have you understand is that the same basic principle applies to the type of energy that you choose to expel as it will nourish or hurt the earth. The earth feeds directly off of the energy that you release. Once you understand this and the true power of what your thoughts and state of being can accomplish, the world will be able to move forward in a new way. Taking true ownership of one's thoughts, actions, and the impact that they have on the collective spirit and the planet is most important. It is not the fear of being punished as many have led you to believe; it is the fact that you hold the means to punish yourselves with what you create that you must fully understand.

Being able to walk the earth and learn the spiritual lessons while being part of the collective spirit is a gift. The ability to watch how the energy shifts and expands is like watching the creation of a tapestry. It is constantly changing with light and feeling, with pleasure and reaction of thought. When people come together to unify over a collective harm, whether it has been caused by the collective release of negative energy or that of an individual who has chosen to turn away from God's path, the result is the same. The healing energy and positive momentum that is created will ultimately cancel out and overcome the original negative energy that was released. How many times do people look to find the good after a disaster? It is the spirit and body self righting the wrong of the situation. It is the collective positive energy canceling out the negative. Most often it starts with just one person. Each one of you has the power to heal, unify and correct imbalances that are taking place in the world. It just takes one to start the shift of the collective energy.

The unity that the world is seeking at this time will be accomplished on an individual basis. Each of you must choose to understand and impart the wisdom of the collective knowledge to each other in ways that make sense to you at this time. It can be as simple as coming together to enforce and impart a feeling of community within your neighbors, schools and nation. Do not leave this up to just those who seem to have the energy in their lives to do this. It is critically important that you each start to understand that you must on an individual basis choose to see how this community of thought and love amongst yourselves is valuable in feeding the world around you. As an individual within the collective you must take the time to make this important and build it into your life. What I mean is that you must figure out what you should be doing with your gift, utilize it, and apply it in a way the community, the world, and the collective can benefit from it. Each of you has been brought to this life with the compassion to do this, just take the time to be silent in mind, body and your surroundings to understand this and then seek to apply it in your own life. Once you are open to this idea God will work with you so that you understand what it is that you as a being can do. The first step is to understand that there is so much more to your life than just what is in front of your eyes.

Part of the balance that we each seek does include the balance within the collective community. First, you must find the balance in yourself between body and spirit and truly acknowledge your gift. It is a continuous journey to keep this balance at all times and God does not expect you to maintain it completely, although, this is the goal we strive for. The struggle to maintain the balance is part of the lessons when you walk this earth. What you need to work towards is applying the concepts laid out thus far. For simplicity sake, and you know I like simplicity, let's try and focus the thoughts:

❖ We are made up of energy that moves freely between the spirit world and the physical world.
❖ Both worlds are bridged by this energy.
❖ We must take ownership of the way in which we move our energy within our body, the collective, the earth and the other dimensions which the energy we release will travel.

❖ God has dispatched beings to help you to assist in your spiritual path and the way in which you use/ shift your energy.

❖ It is our choice to turn away from God's path and our spiritual learning lessons. He will never give up trying to help us return to our path and move forward.

❖ The world is changeable to become what the collective wishes and the shift starts with the energy of each individual. It is simple straight forward and possible.

The individual beings that make up the collective are the means in which to change the very essence of the existence on this earth. They have the power to shape and define the collective, the earth energy, and the power within themselves to do so.

Right now the shift has begun. We know that many of you are coming to this same conclusion and this is being said to other individuals and shown to them with the help of their Guiders and the spirit knowledge that they are able to access by being balanced. Enlightened spirits are being returned to this earth in multiples right now to assist with the changes that are beginning to take place. Many are questioning the notions of the traditional thoughts that have been passed down from generation to generation. The spirits being dispatched at this time are unsettled and wish to explore and understand the spiritual meaning and connection they are feeling and seeing around them. This is by direct design of God. The collective spirits that are returning to the earth are in a larger number of those who are that of a higher spiritual learning level than those younger spirits. In the past it has always been that the younger spirits, those with the most to learn, have outnumbered those who have moved farther on their spiritual journey. This is not so of late, and this inequality of spirit knowledge will continue to grow in this direction. Please do not misunderstand when I say that there are a larger number of spirits returning who are farther along on their spiritual learning, it is just that at this time they are being returned to earth faster than those who are still in their infancy. In addition, we wish to acknowledge that the overall collective spirits have been moving along their spiritual journey at a much more rapid pace than in the past. This is all as it should be considering the amount of work that needs to be done with the changing of the energy releases on the earth.

These changes in the collective will take time; however, the shift has begun and will continue with the spreading and understanding of the power in which each of you was made to wield. The power you have within yourselves and the body vessel that has been gifted to you for this life is the key. No longer should you think that one spirit is not enough to make a change in the way the earth feels and breathes; you alone can make the changes.

CHAPTER FIVE

REFLECTIONS OF HOME

Many techniques have come before to bring personal balance to the space that you reside in, the walls you choose to live within, the placement of items and the colors you choose. It is important that you keep balancing that physical space to bring harmony and peace to your spirit. Each of you has within your thoughts an image of home (where you reside when in spirit form). It is this image that helps to drive you to create and find that sanctuary within this physical world. If you have not been able to tap into that color, fabric or scene that speaks to you, start searching and asking your guides to help you to locate it. We all have it: the reminders of home. It may take a little looking for some to discover it, but when you do, you know that it speaks directly to your being. For some it is not creating it within their home, but spending time in a location that helps their spirit to remember. This maybe in the outdoors, a park, or for some the beauty within a painting or the music from an orchestra. Home has so many aspects and each of you carry a piece within to remind you of the other part of your true existence.

The artists in this world always capture a section from home. This is to help bring that aspect of peace to the physical world. It is the reminder that home exists and a way in which each of you are able to connect to it while not truly understanding the full complexity of what you are seeing and feeling. Art is an expression from the spiritual world. It is a reflection to help you draw strength and support, comfort and knowledge of spirit. The same is true of any creative spirit here on the earth. The works of a creative spirit are helpful reminders to us of what we all remember in home.

We strive to replicate the security, comfort, knowledge and love that exists when we are in our full spirit being. It is the act of finding that balance within ourselves in body form that keeps us seeking the balance within. It is simply how God created us to keep searching for that feeling of completeness when the two are in balance on this earth that is His greatest gift. For by searching to obtain this balance we move forward on our spiritual paths and become closer to that energy being which God moves us to become.

Reminders of home are all around us. We simply need to look with a new set of eyes. Those items, people, tasks, work and simple happiness are all reminders of what we know are from being in complete harmony with ourselves. It is this that helps to motivate us to see the good. When you are able to see beauty in the world or find those things that bring you happiness to your spirit, understand they are glimpses of home. They remind you of the balance that you have when in touch with your spirit-self for you are seeing with your spirit and not your eyes at that moment.

It is easy to become blind to seeing with our spirit eyes. This world has ugliness and darkness and we turn our spirit eyes away when we encounter it. What we should be doing is looking at it more clearly with our spirit eyes to understand how we need to right the injustice with the energy that we create and move out into the world. By turning away from looking at these things with your spirit you are allowing that negativity and hurt to flourish. We have explained that each of you have the ability and the power to change the energy that is cycling on the earth and into the bridge that connects the two parts together and make up the whole of existence. When you allow yourself to see with your spirit eye, you will understand the impact and be able to help cancel out that negative energy flow.

CHAPTER SIX

THE TRUE WORLD & FAITH

So much has been written and expressed about the "two worlds:" the spiritual and the physical. It is time to cast off that thought process all together. The spiritual beings on the earth now must accept, acknowledge, and begin the thought process of understanding that there are not two worlds. This concept was important for many life cycles for spirits to move forward. It was easier in their learning process to think of the two as separate and segregated because the enormity of the fact that the two are one was not readily able for the majority to grasp. They needed to accept that the two existed, but the leap to the belief that they are in fact the same was outside of their collective grasp.

With the openness of spiritual awareness and science understanding that there is more than just what the physical eye can see we can now explain the true world in hopes that you will start to accept it as knowledge. Just as God has created you to have the physical and spiritual within yourself that must be balanced for you to whole, He created the physical existence and the spiritu existence to be combined as whole, as well. The true worl existence lies within the combination of both the physical earth and the spiritual energy together. Without either part, the ability to move forward and become those beings which God created us to be would not be possible. It is important that each of you realize you are responsible for both parts of the true world in order for the balance and existence in either to be of full possibility. Both halves of the whole need to be able to co-exist in order for the full movement of self to take place. Just asking you to understand this and apply it in to your thought patterns, physical understanding, and spirit is enormous. It is simple and you will see that it is the other side of the equation that is needed at this moment in time.

The movement of the energies back and forth is like the blood flowing to nourish your cells. The energy flow between the two halves is the spiritual blood that is required in true world existence. This energy is what nourishes both parts. The importance of keeping it pure, nourished, and in balance within the two halves is the key to keeping the balance of the true world. It is not just the earth that is being fed by the energy release and how that energy is used by the collective; it is that which sustains the whole. This concept is bigger than most of you wish to acknowledge and we understand this because it means that the enormity and responsibility that each of you have is not just to yourself, the earth, but also to all of the beings in spirit and in physical form.

When you acknowledge and accept that the two are .e, then your ability to move energies within are endless. The connection that the two can be utilized together, like your body and spirit, can help you to understand the impossible accomplishments that take place. Why some individuals seem to be able to move through adversity with ease of peace and the knowledge that they will come to the other side of it in harmony even though they do not know what lies ahead. Their ability to walk through the world with what you call faith. These spirits who walk with the balance and faith are able to tap in to the combined energies of both. They understand that there is the bridge between that connects the two parts into a whole being. It is the concept and understanding of the whole being which allows faith to exist. God does not impart a specific energy for faith. It is within all of us. It is the ability to understand the feeling of balance that is obtained within the spirit-self and body self. When we understand that state and we are moved out of it because of a struggle or a choice, then faith is the knowledge that at some point in the future that balance will be obtained again; that its existence is tangible and with the grace of God we will find it again. It is the understanding that God wishes us to find that balance and has created us to have it. It is up to us to allow it to come into full existence.

When people declare that they do not have any faith, it is just that they have not found the balance within of their spirit-self. Some may be able to utilize the gift that God has given to them in this life and can be successful on earth; however, they do not understand why they have that gift or for what purpose it was given. They utilize it without ever

understanding the full potential of it within the true wo...
context. Some enter this world with the feeling that ther
is more and are able to accept it without any proof. This
is also another example of what you call faith. What they
accept is that there are two parts to the true world that they
are flowing and moving together and that just because they
are unable to see that other half that it does exist. Many just
label this as having faith in the existence of God. This is the
simplest way to think of it.

What we are attempting to show you is the vastness of
the true world and how it all relates so that you can be more
full beings and participants in the actual world that exists.
That you not only exist in, but are able to affect both parts
of the world that you reside in. Just because you are not
in full spirit form, that you are connected with your body
vessel, do not make the mistake of thinking that you are
not also residing within the spirit part of the world at the
same time. You are. You are able to feel, see and respond to
those in true spirit state. God has made you part of both. It
is the ability to live within the two that puts you in balance.
This is a concept that many are starting to understand and
discuss. It is different, but you will find that it makes perfect
sense. Faith is the belief and understanding that this state
exists and trusting that God is empowering us all and is a
part of our constant existence.

God wishes us to experience both halves of the world
to become complete. The learning and existing that we
have while in body form provides us with the ability to
open ourselves up to the spirit side of the world. It enables
us to understand concepts and implement them in ways
that we would not be able to in spirit form. The ability to

derstand that we have a limited existence in body form llows for the true necessity to live a full and rich existence while here. Understanding that we will continue after we leave our body vessel enables us to be comforted at the loss of a loved one.

CHAPTER SEVEN

BEING HUMBLE

Once you begin to grasp the amount of power and energy control that you have while in this existence, it is hard not to become over-powered with the belief that you are entitled to move things into being that you wish. It is important that you understand that humility takes on a new meaning at this stage. You are able to choose and control the thoughts, actions, and energy movement in your daily lives. This requires a choice of great control and focus. This does not mean that you are not able to make mistakes. In order to understand completely your ability to call things into being and generate cellular health, you must learn how to utilize it. Your thoughts and actions should always be in alignment with your spiritual path and the greater good (the good of the true world and that of the earth). If this is not the case, then it will not come into being. It also must not cause any universal harm. When you make a request of the true world energy you must be aware of what you are fully asking, how it will impact the greater good, and what goal will be attained by its end. These are the same principles that apply what is commonly thought of as prayer. Both are just the simple asking of God.

When you tell a child to be "true to yourself," you are asking them to call upon their own knowledge of spirit-self and apply it outwardly. Each of us has the ability to understand what we need in this life at an early age. The younger we are the easier it is to see what those core items are. As we grow and become more engrossed in the physical world, we lose that connection. In fact, we spend most of our time trying to capture that pure understanding of ourselves again during the remainder of our life cycle. We have already described how a child is closer to their spirit-self and how we are able to see that when we look at them. In this same way, they understand a better balance between the physical and the spiritual. They have a built-in balance within that starts to fade with the challenges that we face in this life time. It is important to help nurture children to keep that sense of self as long as possible. The innocence and wonder that they have from the moment they arrive is merely the ability to see the aspects of the spirit side combined with that of the physical. You can say that they are truly seeing with both their spirit eyes and physical eyes. This is what God is asking you to do in your life. See both parts of the world, feel both parts, and make choices according to the understanding of both. We have all experienced this at one time in our lives and it is this true seeing that we are asked to try and find over and over again. For it is through the experience of life and the ability that God has given us to grow and expand our spirits in knowledge that provides the gifts that we search for.

Humility comes from an understanding of the re that you play within the true world. We have been given the gift of life in the physical and the spiritual. Stop and think about all of the assistance, guidance and love that has been provided to you as one being. You are able to access both sides and live within both. You are offered the ability to know the world in a new way and touch the lives of beings on both sides. You have within you the choice to understand the magnitude of your actions and thoughts and choose what you wish to do. The understanding that you are offered this choice and told no matter what God will keep moving to help you to understand the balance and love that is all around you. That you are able to move forward as you are willing and able. That you are loved to such a point that Guiders, Spirit Guides and Guardians have been sent to help you. These things alone should humble you. God loves each of us to such an extreme level that he helps us to discover our paths, plan and make free choices on an endless basis. These are the simple truths that one must always remember even while battling deep lessons. Keep them close at hand to help move you to see the greater world around you. The choice has always been yours and always will be yours as to how you move through the world. Take the time to connect with your spirit-self, find your true balance within both parts of the world, and welcome the lessons that you need to learn in this life to move you forward. It is simple in the process, but difficult in the learning, if you choose it to be. God loves us enough to let us choose.

CHAPTER EIGHT

ATTAINING BALANCE

The most difficult part in attaining the balance in spirit-self and body vessel is learning to get out of our own way. We have all been given the tools within ourselves to find this balance and harmony; however, we have a way of choosing not to listen. Luckily, we have been blessed with beings to help us to remember. That is all we are doing, working to remember the knowledge that we already have. How many times have you felt happy, content, blessed, loved and at rest within your body and heart? When you are in that place, it feels like home, doesn't it? A peacefulness that you feel is right, correct, effortless and natural. This is because at that time you are in the presence of full balance and this is where God allows us to find home again. Home is a place we can visit anytime we wish once we understand how to obtain this balance between the physical and spiritual: the place that energy is flowing freely from both sides and you are able to be in complete contact with it.

If you have not been able to experience this within yourself, you may have felt it by way of a life event that has brought it to you. The birth of a child, the view from the mountain top, the spirit of a loved one, the satisfaction of completing a work utilizing a gift that God has provided you with. There are endless ways that we are shown this within our hearts that touch our spirits. It is at these times that we begin to understand what balance feels like. Simply put, it is when we are feeling and seeing with both the physical and the spiritual side of our being. This is the place that we each need to be and the place we should make choices from. The ability to come into balance is something that we have within ourselves and must find by ourselves. You must understand that NO ONE other than ourselves can bring us to this place. It is not the responsibility of any other being on earth or in spirit to move us to this place of balance. They can help to guide us and show us the way, but only you can bring this to yourself. You cannot receive it from another.

All too often we make the mistake of thinking that we will obtain this peace by having the right amount of money in the bank, the right partner in this life, or the right job. These are all things that can bring joy on a physical level; however, they will never bring you to the place of balance and peace within yourself that you seek. That resides in you and no other earthly item will move you into this state of being. Once you accept that you have the power and answers within yourself to bring this to yourself, then you can take the first steps to achieving it. Just as God has provided animals with the ability to keep this balance, He has provided you with the ability to find it again in this life.

The first step is accepting that there is another part of this life that is unseen by your physical eye. Realize that you are more than just the vessel that you move in at this

oment and that you have a deeper part that is spirit, which
.s more than just the cells that you inhabit. That this part is
uniquely you, unlike anyone that has been created before,
and that you alone and God are the only beings that are
able to truly understand and know your spirit. We will share
our spirit with many beings, but none will understand the
full potential and abilities of your spirit, but you and God.
Take comfort in knowing that even when we are discovering
who we truly are God already knows and is waiting for you
to discover the beauty, uniqueness and love that is you.
He already knows you because you are His creation and is
patiently awaiting your reunion with yourself.

Once you have accepted this simple truth, then the
door can begin to open for you. Now it is time for you to
bridge the distance in your mind from one side to the other
and join them together as one. This is the balance. Your
thoughts have power. They can move you forward in your
true world existence. It is settling down and directing them
that requires practice. Simple meditation is so important
to most of you. The quieting of the mind, the control of
body, and the accessing of spirit can be developed with
meditation. Many beings have worked to help the collective
to understand the value and necessity of meditation. It is not
something that we feel at this time needs to be discussed
in great detail. Just know that this is an important key for
many of you to find and sustain the balance between body
vessel and spirit. It is not the only technique used, but it
is up to the individual to find what quiets the body and
allows the spirit to be heard. Each person knows what that
is and it varies drastically from individual. For some it is
the feeling and connection after great exertion, for others it

is the feeling when they have spent time outdoors or in the presence of great art or music. Each of you knows what this is and should make time daily to bring it into your existence. It is finding that one thing that feeds your spirit and allows you to focus your thoughts on a peaceful fluid energy flow. Water is a good source to assist you. If you do not have access to a large body of water, simply just place a bowl in your home. Watching the movement as you touch it or the simple stillness of the water will help to quiet your energy. All of your time in physical form you have been surrounded and in touch with water. Use it to comfort your being. Look at it as a tool to assist you and not just something that is required in this body form to be healthy.

We understand that for some this is not a comfortable place to be because it is so unknown and foreign at first. That you doubt that this simple act of being quiet and still will be counterproductive to what you feel you must do to move you forward. It is so vastly the opposite. It is through being quiet and opening the door between the two halves of the world that you move forward. Only by being present within the two are you able to fulfill the work that you have come here to do. When you begin this work be certain to ask for help from the beings that God has sent to assist you. They will be able to make the connection once you ask. Again, we cannot stress how much this has to be your decision to move forward with your learning of the true world and the energy balance that you command. It is the seeking of one's self and the knowledge that you have within. When you move with the knowledge of the two halves as one and the ability to allow yourself to consider how your thoughts will impact both, then you will begin to find your path that has been laid out for you to follow.

Once you have identified what you require to feel the connection to your spirit and the sensation of peace that it brings, you must start to create your life on earth to replicate this so it will become a more effortless state for you to find. You will always be pulled away from this balance by the circumstances taking place on and in the earth, but you need to have the presence of mind to move back to the place of balance.

Begin by creating your dwelling to ensure that it brings that peace and balance to you. Remember color, texture, scents, art and music are all glimpses of spiritual home and it is important that you surround yourself with these memories. If you are not gifted to do this yourself, then seek another who can assist you. Do not worry about finding the right items or colors you will know what speaks to your spirit and brings that sense for warmth, love and peace.

All too often people do not realize that their physical home here does not need to be much, but it does need to bring them peace and joy. It is the location that we all go to: to replenish, rejuvenate and nourish ourselves. If this space is disruptive to any of these goals, we will not be able to be balanced in the way we need to be to stay healthy. What you should try and focus your energy on is to let go of all the stress, anxiety and sense of urgency that you have taken on during your time away from home. Release it from your being, as when you open the window to change the air within a room. Your physical home needs to be a place of sanctuary for you and those you choose to allow in. This is something that is said over and over again, but many do not

take the time to make it so. It is an important part in be
able to maintain a balance. For each person this will mea
something totally different. Some are more comfortable
with disorganization; others will choose the opposite. It does
not matter, it is what makes you feel at ease and peaceful.
You are responsibile to do this for yourself and not for any
other individual. It is important that you understand that
we each need to have things around us that speak to our
spiritual side and that you must allow others who live within
your home to have those things close to them that speak
to their spirit. This goes back to our earlier discussion on
compromise being a gift to all. Always keep this in mind
when someone allows you into their home. Be kind and
respectful of their sanctuary and the glimpses of their spirit
that they are allowing you to see. Never be judgmental for
how can you presume to know what their spirit needs.

As you begin to explore the depths of your being in
the way that God has set out for you the immeasurable
feeling of connection and understanding will move you to
share and express this to others. It may not be a conscious
choice for your energy will change it and you will become
a beacon that others around you will see and be drawn to
it. This is by design and something that is truly wonderful.
You have all seen it and felt it in others around you. This
balance does not come from any other source than yourself.
Once you realize this, that all you need is within you, and
the earth around you it will become easier. There is no
secret, no complex equation. It is just allowing yourself
to be in the full presence of yourself. Remember, God has
designed you to be able to do this, so, do not think that you
are unable to; however, know that this is a choice that you

st decide to make for without making that decision you
ll never find this balance. That is the most misunderstood
principle of learning. God has given us the ability to choose
throughout our entire existence. Without this ability we
would never move forward or discover who we truly are.
This is the strongest struggle we have within. We have the
choice to balance our spirit and body vessel. We have the
choice to walk the spiritual path of learning or turn away
from it. Yes, we do have wonderfully loving and creative
beings around us to help. Do not make the mistake that
they will do the work in making us achieve our goals in this
lifetime: it is always a choice. What you must do to receive
the most amount of help from God and those He has sent
to assist you in this life is to allow them to work with you.
How do you do this? It is simple. Ask them for help and
guidance. For when you acknowledge them and join your
energy with theirs, it allows for greater flow of energy to
help you. Yes, no matter what, they are helping to guide
you. Even those of you who have no idea they exist; but,
now that you understand energy movement, apply that to
the knowledge that combining your energy with those of
your Spirit Guides, Guiders and Guardian will bring that
much more into being.

Now that you understand how important it is that you
work in connection with those who God has empowered to
assist you in this life cycle you have no reason not to ask for
help. A constant through the ages of man has been the need
to understand that you require help in this life and being
humble enough to ask for assistance. It is ironic how God
created us to need the humility to ask for help. So many
of us are unable to do this. We find it nearly impossible. It

is easy to help another or see how you can aide them, b
when it comes to ourselves we do not see the need. Man
of us jump to the aide of those in need, first responders,
doctors, nurses, teachers and parents, but we forget how to
take care of the most important thing – ourselves. For if we
are not balanced and nourished, we are not able to truly help
anyone. The way of the world today does not allow for this
to come naturally. It has almost been made achievable for
those with the monetary wealth to take the time to spend
on oneself. This attitude must be stopped. Take the time to
allow yourself to be taken care of by those who know you
best, you and those whom God has sent to help you. It does
not take long periods of time during the day. It is having the
presence of mind to take the moments to be still, reflective
and listen to the earth around you, the spirit within and
the energy moving in between. The greatest thing that you
can do for those who love you is to become the person that
you truly are. One who is able to balance the energy within
yourself, your home, the community, the earth and the
collective.

The understanding of what this feels like is not what
is difficult: it is working every moment of every day to
stay in this place of being, that is. It is the changing of the
thought patterns, the realizing that you can put yourself
first, but at the same time being responsible for not creating
a negative ripple to the community, earth and collective
by being selfish. We all bear a great responsibility to the
true world and it starts with our own being and moves
outward to reach all things in this life cycle and those
beyond. Do not presume to understand all of the world
that God has created, for you are only seeing a simple part.

there are much more complex areas to the physical world that you are not in contact with yet. As the collective spirit advances, those other physical areas will be shown to you. Understanding each one is not necessary, but the knowing that they exist and that your choices directly impact them is something that you must understand and start thinking of in your existence.

We have touched on the fact that your thoughts have power. Any type of power is a responsibility and needs to be looked at as to how it will impact all of those beings on each side of the true world. If you focus your thoughts on the negative, you will draw more negative to you. Like energy attracts like energy. This is how things begin to grow so easily among the collective. Just because you are immersed around other beings that may be in a negative learning cycle at a moment, it does not mean that you take on their energy and bring it into yours. It is your choice to do so. Positive energy cancels out the negative energy and starts a shift. This is what you must remember and take action. It is important not to allow those around you to influence your energy or your path. Part of being balanced is having the ability to know yourself. What you must do to keep moving forward on the learning process you are here for and to recognize when you are being pulled off that course.

We can support those around us without being caught up in their own path. This is the easiest thing to see when watching others, but the hardest when it comes to ourselves. We think we are helping another along their path when, in actuality, we are being pulled away from our own and inhibiting their ability to learn the lessons that they are here for. The best thing we can do is allow them to walk their path and experience the bumps along the way while being a cheerleader from the side. We must understand that we can be supportive without attempting to directly take control of their path. Again, it is having the ability to be in a state that we can see the full picture. Finding a way to provide them with the tools they need while at the same time allowing them to choose which one to use and when. Have faith in the knowledge that they, like you, are being guided and moved according to a direction that has been agreed upon. You are in their life for a reason, but not to do their work for them. You have your own, and if you are doing theirs you have put aside your own.

It is connecting the two sides of the world together that will help you in being able to allow someone who you are in contact with walk their own path. Understanding that it takes both sides working together to move someone forward. That there is more working to assist them than just you. Trusting that they will be able to make the best decisions for themselves, even if it is part of a learning lesson being taught in such a way that you are seeing something that you do not wish for that other individual. Realizing that you do not truly know what is best for their spiritual development and trusting that God will continue to work and move with them no matter what choices they make. Spiritual growth, like any, is not always an easy process. It is hard work and not everyone takes the same path. Watching someone going through it is not easy, but knowing that it is for a greater purpose, one which the person in spirit form helped to develop, assists in the witnessing.

As you evolve on your spiritual journey, it becomes clear to see what lessons others are here to learn. It is much more difficult to see your own. This is one of the reasons why we choose to come to physical form with the same spirits over and over again. We develop a strong connection to them through the life cycle and in spirit form. We work together to help propel each other to the next level of understanding. These relationships can be easy or hard. Many times the individual who frustrates you in physical form helps to move you forward on your path more than anyone else that you encounter. Usually, the reason why is something that you are unwilling to face. That they are bringing out a deficit you have in your spiritual learning, one in which you are not ready to acknowledge. Typically, the learning is about you and not about them. When you encounter such a being make sure to take time and step back to understand why this person bothers you so much. Remember that you control your own energy and how your energy reacts to that individual. They are feeding off of what you produce and send towards them, so if you change your energy release around them, you may just find that it changes everything.

It is not easy to stop and look at an aspect of yourself that you are not comfortable with. In this life it is much easier to put the blame or disappointment in a relationship onto the other being. That it is a deficit that they have and that you are not a part of, one in which that other person needs to work on. The truth is that you must take a look and accept your reaction to that person and not what they must do to be better. Look at how your body, spirit and energy react to that individual. Then, coming from a place of balance, focus on why you react so strongly to that situation or individual. This is the hard work we have come here to do. Moving to that state in which we are able to look at ourselves and find out what makes us respond in this life and working choose how we react and not just to react. Like all growth this requires energy, balance and the ability to be willing to own our personal actions. We must be humble enough to know that we are here to learn and that we are not at the end of our learning cycle and embrace the ability that God has given us to keep learning. Yes, it is exhausting at times, but that is when you must have the presence of spirit to ask for help. The beings that are ready to assist us do not care how small or big the request is. It is the act of asking that is the important action.

There are so many instances that require a place of balance in order to move forward. When you stop and think about how many times a conversation, a task or an event went smoother when you have taken the time to be still, contemplate and take out what the other factors are, and simply look at your own ability to respond to the situation, you realize quickly that the end result was much better than if you had just acted. It is taking the time to look at all sides of the equation, the pattern and the collective. Once you have done this and are coming from that balanced place which is combined of spirit and body, then you are able to make decisions that will benefit all. Nothing grows quickly in this physical world, it takes time nourishment, and patience. Think of this when you are reacting in a situation or dealing with another. To allow for growth we must be patient and make sure that we are nourishing the situation in the correct way. In doing this we allow for the time to consider, reflect, and respond in the best possible way for the greater good. This world has evolved in such a fast pace of wanting to have everything today, that moment, instant munication, that it has forgotten the simple rules of e. Things grow slowly and at their own pace of being. You cannot nor ever should you expect someone to grow at your pace or to try to hurry them on their path. It will take as long as they need it to. The flower takes as long as it needs to receive all the energy, nourishment and strength to open. We can help it along with the environmental needs that it requires, but the work is up to the flower and its energy. The same is true with you. It is important that you take control over your own physical vessel, provide for it, and in the same way do those things that feed the connection to your spirit. In doing so you provide what you need to grow. No one knows how fast that growth will be except for God. It is up to you to keep the water flowing in, the sun shining, and the energy pure. This is your responsibility alone; but never forget that you have all of those beings helping you with the spiritual side which connects with the physical. Others will help to guide and teach you, but the work is for you alone to do. Understanding and accepting that this is what we are here to do will allow you to become balanced.

CHAPTER NINE

GUIDERS (ANGELS)

We have already described how Guiders have been created by God to assist you along your path here on earth. What we have not shared is how that they also assist you while in true spirit form. Their tasks and missions are direct and simple, but cover a vast amount of knowledge and skillsets. This is one of the reasons why they have always been Guiders and never walked in physical form as you and I have. Their energy is light and pure allowing for the easy movement within both sides of the true world. Guiders are complete healers of body and spirit. They replenish us whenever we need it, cleanse our body vessel of negative energy, and help to motivate us in our work here on earth. At times, they work in groups to allow us to benefit from their assistance and move us along on our path. They provide us with the ability to tap into the faith that we have when it is waning because of difficulties on our path. Guiders provide assistance in finding that connection with our spirit side. In actuality, they are the energy beings that are the "jacks of all trades." They do whatever is required to aide us in this life cycle. It can be physical healing, emotional healing or simply helping us to understand and connect to our full selves. A Guider's entire existence is about helping a spirit to move forward on their learning process.

Their work with us continues while we are in spirit form. When at home and working on reviewing what we need to learn to move forward on our spiritual path, they are there beside us to inspire us as to how we can best utilize the energy of the time period we are considering to come back in, and those other spirits we should be connecting with during that life cycle. They have an uncanny ability to help pair spirits together. Once a Guider has felt that two spirits should be connected together in a learning process, they start to weave the connection between the two even in spirit form. This is a beautiful thing to watch and experience. It is not just the colors that are being woven, but the energy field between the two. This is one of the most wondrous things to witness. When you become connected with your body form, then this connection becomes hidden from you until you encounter that spirit in body form. This is something that is used to help move beings forward. It may be simply the connection to an animal spirit, a child, a spouse or a parent. It can take on any combination.

If the Guider, for the good of all, and with the consent of both spirits feels it is appropriate they sever this connection when you take physical form. This will begin the process of the spirits to search for this connection again because they know that in order for them to each be complete they must be connected with the other spirit. Understand that this is not used with every person, it is in select cases. Most often this bond is used to help us with recognizing significant

people along our path and it is not severed when you com.
to physical form. It allows you to realize that this spirit you
have encountered is significant to you. We all recognize
spirits that we have been with in another life journey. This
is not the same as when a Guider bonds the two spirits
together. This is the actual intertwining of energies and is
not done lightly. It is a tool that propels spirits along quickly
and intensely. So, when you encounter someone in your path
that you have known before, who understands you on a very
deep level, remember that you have a Guider to thank for
helping to strengthen that connection with that spirit and
that you have both chosen to be connected in this learning
cycle and at home.

In addition to helping to pair spirits and assist in the
planning stages of a learning life cycle, they work with those
who are lost on their path on earth. When a person is in
great need and lost, they come to assist.

Guider (*Angel*) - We are dispatched to help in any means
necessary. Each Guider has a specific mission with each
spirit. We try to stay with the person for as long as possible.
The work that must be completed has to be done by the
spirit we are there to encourage, empathize and provide
extra energy to move along what the spirit has started. We
never create, change or influence the choices of a spirit. We
simply help see that what they have started with the choices
that they make for the greater good and their selves move
forward easily. When they question a choice and if it is for
the good, we help them to reseed the doubt that they have
in their selves. We provide comfort in decisions that have
been made for the good of that spirit, the collective, and
the community. If they have chosen a negative solution, we

y to show them the way gently back to balance. Our job
s to never judge, harm or bear false witness to a spirit. God
did not weave those things into our being. By now, you
should understand that those things are choices for spirits
in bodily form. We do not have those choices. Our mission
is simple: we work for the good of the spirit and that of the
overall universal order within which we inhabit and work.
May I say, that we are truly excited that we have the ability
to show and tell you that we are more than just rescuing
beings; that we are side by side with you working for all. We
do not sit and watch. We are active participants in the true
world and that we, as well as all beings, bear witness to your
growth individually and collectively; that we derive great
satisfaction in our work of being helpful beings. This is what
moves us forward: understanding that we can help you. This
is the simple state of our being. We have the ability to do so
much with your permission and your ability to understand
your true fit within the combined true world. You can reach
for the stars as you live among them whether it be in body
form or in spirit form. All is one celestial body and you
have the ability to work within both at once. We are proof
of that…our ability to work with you on both sides of the
world. You need to utilize us in our full capacity and we are
so excited to do so. Just ask and we shall help you, we love
you, you are our brothers and sisters. We may have different
purposes, but we are one family. Please start thinking of us
in that way. All of us are one family working together.

CHAPTER TEN

THE END AS THE BEGINNING

As you learn more and more about the true world and how energy moves freely between the physical vessel and the spirit form, you start to understand that there is never an end; only a movement to the other part of the world or your full life. Think of your full life as an endless circle moving from spirit form to body vessel and back again. Remember that you are always connected to both and that when you leave the physical world you are simply shedding the vessel that you have used to help move you forward on your spiritual journey like a tool. It is just this simple. You will encounter those spirits who you have been wishing to see, understand the full knowledge that your spirit contains and begin the review and excitement of embracing the knowledge that you have gained during your life cycle on earth. These are all joys that should be looked at as just that. When a loved one takes the journey back to spirit form without us, it is important to understand that they are completing a learning journey of their own and that their departing before us is an opportunity for us to move forward on our own path. It is not easy; learning is an exercise in growth, and growth can come in many forms. The connections that you forge with people during your life cycle will continue into the other half of the true world. You will still remain connected. That does not change. It is a constant. There will be moments of grief and despair. This is when it is most important that you turn to those whom God has entrusted to help you in the physical realm and the spiritual. Why do you think He has provided help for you in both areas? Isn't it clear that you reside in both and thus require help from both? Do not dismiss your yearnings and desires to understand that there is much more to existing than just the physical. Your spirit is calling for you to understand do not turn away from it.

When it is time for you to return to spirit form you have choices to make. There are those who feel as though their work in the physical realm is not completed, that they can do more by being in spirit form than in the physical at that point in time. They then choose to stay with those still in physical form that they were connected to. This is up to that spirit. It could be a parent who wishes to continue to help, guide and assist their child as if they were still in physical form. Many times a spirit will choose to leave their physical vessel because they feel as though they are no longer able to move forward on their path or that if they are in spirit form they will have more freedom to help another. This is the choice of the spirit. A spirit who has newly shed its body vessel is still very much tied to the physical realm and is able to use its energy clearly to connect with those still in body form. The energy they have is very strong and easily felt. Other spirits will choose to move quickly to the spirit side of the world in order to revisit the learning they have just completed to truly comprehend what they have experienced. What you must remember is that we have the freedom to choose in both places.

If a spirit chooses to stay close to those still in body form, they are able to help those they wish in ways that are similar to those who God has entrusted with guiding you during your time on earth. Please do not make the mistake of thinking that the spirit who has just moved from body form to spirit form becomes your guider. They do not. However, they can stay with you and help you with healing, comfort, assist you in developing a gift that God has given to you and help in so many other ways. This is a choice that the spirit has.

Your ability to make choices and choose how you will continue to learn and develop your spirit does not just reside in the physical side. It is a constant within the whole true world. Remember that what God has given to you in physical form, the freedom of choice, the ability to learn, and affect other beings, still continues in the spirit side as well. As we have said before, you need to expand your understanding of the world and its principles of energy movement into the spiritual. Stop and think how easy it is to understand when you connect the two together and see the world under one large umbrella encompassing both sides. We all reside in one world. We are all together, and combined as one family. God did not just create your spirit, but ours as well. He never meant for us to be separated and we never have. It is just that it has taken time for the spiritual development of the collective to come to a place in which we could start laying the foundation for the truth about your true life, true world, and true family.

GLOSSARY

God – we *(the spirits writing this book)* do not refer to any man made religion, culture or mindset - it does not matter. It is simply however you think of the creator of the universe. It makes no difference. They are infact, all one and the same.

Spirit Guides – beings in spirit form whom God has dispatched to assist a specific spirit in body vessel form in learning spiritual lessons during a life cycle.

Guardian – being created by God with a sole purpose to guard and protect a spirit every moment during their life cycle, so they may move freely along the path they have chosen.

Guider – being created by God whom have never been in body vessel form and are dispatched to help spirits in any way necessary, in either body or spirit form.

Balance – the state of being wherein you have attributes of both your physical being and your spiritual being. The place where you are able to have equal flow of energy between your spirit energy and physical energy.

Body Vessel – a tool which God has provided us with to use in order to move along our spiritual path of learning.

<u>Collective</u> - the combination of all the spirits in body form on the earth.

<u>Earth</u> - a whole being entity that God created to assist us while on this spiritual journey He has set forth. It reflects the notions, movement and attributes that the collective energies inhabiting it are feeling.

<u>Energy Power</u> - the energy that God has provided you with while in body form. It is that energy you command in personal thought and personal action.

<u>Full Life</u> – the movement from spirit form to body vessel and back again to spirit form.

<u>Greater Good</u> - the good of the true world and that of the earth.

<u>Home</u> - where you reside when in spirit form.

<u>Spirit Form</u> - the exact state of being in which God has created us.

<u>True World</u> - the physical world and the spiritual world combined equally.

TRUE WORLD

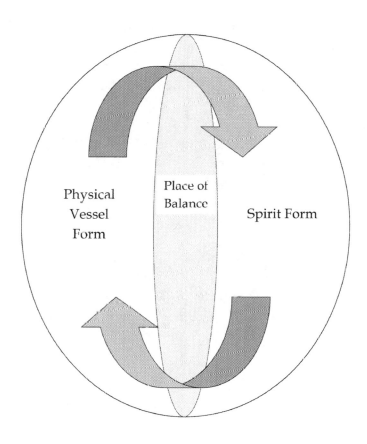

Physical Vessel Form

Place of Balance

Spirit Form

ABOUT THE AUTHOR

Heather has spent her whole life in the Greater Boston area in Massachusetts. Her gift to see and feel the spirit side of the True World was revealed to her at an early age. After the birth of her autistic son, her gift had grown and she became able to channel from the spirit side. She began working with individuals to help them receive messages and guidance from their respective Spirit Guides and other beings whom God had placed around them. Over time, Heather's Spirit Guides "encouraged" her with urgency to channel three books. *The Truth of Life* is the first book. Heather continues to channel for individuals and groups as she works on the remaining books.

Printed in the United States
By Bookmasters